D1055047

George Washington

YEARLING BOOKS are designed especially to entertain and enlighten young people. The finest available books for children have been selected under the direction of Charles F. Reasoner, Professor of Elementary Education, New York University.

For a complete listing of all Yearling titles,
write to Education Sales Department, Dell Publishing Co., Inc.
1 Dag Hammarskjold Plaza, New York, N.Y. 10017

George Washington
Father of Freedom

by Stewart Graff

illustrated by Robert Doremus

A YEARLING BOOK

This book is for
Kate Graff,
with love

Published by
DELL PUBLISHING CO., INC.
1 Dag Hammarskjold Plaza
New York, N.Y. 10017

Copyright © 1960 by Anne Colver
ISBN:0-440-42858-0
All rights reserved.
Reprinted by arrangement with Garrard Publishing Company.
Printed in U. S. A.

Ninth Dell Printing—May 1980

GEORGE WASHINGTON is one of the *Discovery* biographies
published by Garrard Publishing Co., Champaign, Illinois.
Discovery books are published by Garrard in library bindings.

This book is one of a series of educational,
informative biographies, presented in a lively,
colorful and interesting manner. They are designed
and edited so that they can be read and
enjoyed by young readers through the elementary
grades. All facts are authentic for they have
been carefully checked with leading sources for
historical accuracy.

Contents

George Washington: Father of Freedom

Chapter *1*

Storm

Thunder rolled over the green Virginia hills. Lightning flashed against the black clouds. It was a spring afternoon in the year 1744.

Twelve-year-old George Washington sat easily on the big gray horse. He watched the dark clouds coming nearer. His horse began to move restlessly. George patted the big animal's neck.

"Quiet, Gray," he said. Gray had been his father's horse. George loved to ride him.

Suddenly George remembered another spring, Eastertime a year ago. He had been away from home visiting cousins. A swift rider brought the news that George's father was very sick. In a few days he was dead. George still missed him. His father had taught him to ride over the broad, rolling Virginia fields.

There was another clap of thunder. The big gray horse shied. George's legs tightened around the frightened animal.

"Race the storm, Gray," he cried, and they were off at full gallop. But the rain came pelting down long before they reached the shelter of the barn.

As George swung down from the saddle he saw another wet horse.

"Lawrence is here," he shouted. In a moment his long legs were flying as he ran to find his older brother.

Lawrence was standing in the dining room. His younger brothers and sisters were crowding around, but Lawrence looked especially at George.

"You have grown another inch," he said. "You are almost big enough to be a planter." Lawrence turned to George's mother. "May George come home with me for a visit?" he asked.

"I can be ready in five minutes," George answered happily.

His mother laughed. "Tomorrow will be time enough," she said. "You both have to dry out."

It was a long ride the next day. Lawrence and his wife, Nancy, lived in a big house called Mount Vernon. It looked down over the wide Potomac River. George liked the lively, friendly life there. Lawrence was fourteen years older than he was. He seemed almost like another father.

George and Lawrence rode together every day. Once they stopped at the top of a high hill. Lawrence pointed far ahead. "Away to the west are miles and miles of forest," he said. "Someday it will be farms and towns."

Chapter 2

The Young Soldier

During the next few years, George often visited Lawrence. Lawrence was a planter. He was also a soldier. He taught young soldiers of Virginia how to drill and fight. Like the other American colonies, Virginia was ruled by England. But she had her own soldiers.

"Someday I want to be a soldier," George told Lawrence.

Lawrence smiled. "Let's think about school right now," he said.

George was sent to school in Fredericksburg, near his mother's farm. He worked hard at his studies. He was also learning many things on his visits to Mount Vernon. Lawrence taught him how to grow tall corn and wheat and tobacco. George learned to saddle a wild young horse. He learned to camp in the woods and to hunt. He was proud of his gun.

When George finished school, he said to Lawrence, "I want to be a surveyor."

"I think that would be good work for you," Lawrence said. "I know surveyors in Fredericksburg who can teach you."

George worked hard. He learned to measure small plots of land for town houses. He learned to measure and map hundreds of acres in the wilderness. Landowners liked his work.

George still went to Mount Vernon often. Colonel Fairfax lived nearby. Pretty Sally Fairfax helped teach George to dance. Sally put her small slipper next to George's big foot. "Now step," she said. *"Step!"* The family laughed as tall young George struggled to learn. George laughed too.

Mount Vernon had always been a happy place for George. But it became a place of sadness too. When George was 20, Lawrence died. George could take care of himself, but he missed his happy older brother.

George became a successful surveyor. After Lawrence died, Mount Vernon became his home.

George liked having his own land. "But someone must take my brother Lawrence's place training the soldiers," George said. "I believe I can do it." So he went to see the Governor.

Governor Dinwiddie liked the calm steadiness in George's eyes. He felt a quiet power in the younger man.

"You are only 20," the Governor said. "But I will give you the chance."

George became Major George Washington of the Virginia militia.

Chapter 3

A Dangerous Ride

One day Governor Dinwiddie sent for George. "I have bad news," he said. "Indian traders say the French are building forts in the Ohio country."

The rich Ohio country was land to the west. Both England and France claimed it.

"England must control the Ohio country," Governor Dinwiddie said to George. "It is rich land. Take this letter to the French commander. It tells him he must leave."

On a cold November day George set out on the long ride. There were seven men in his party. One of them was Christopher Gist, a woodsman and guide. The men rode over the rough mountain trails to the Ohio country.

"We had rains, snows and bad traveling through many miles," George wrote. Two friendly Indian chiefs named Half King and White Thunder helped them find the way.

At last they reached the French fort. George gave his letter to the French commander. The commander was polite to George, but his answer was firm.

"This country belongs to France," the commander said. "No Englishman can even trade here."

George told Christopher, "We must warn the Governor. The French will build new forts in the spring."

The trip back was hard and slow. The weather grew worse. *"Our horses were weak and feeble. They grew less able to travel every day,"* George wrote later. George knew he must hurry. "I decided to take the nearest way through the woods on foot."

George and Christopher left the others to follow. They hurried on alone. It was hard walking. The snow was deep.

There were other troubles. *"In a place called the Murdering Town, Indians had lain in wait for us,"* George wrote. "One of them fired, but fortunately missed. We walked all the rest of the night to be out of reach."

Finally they came to the broad Allegheny River. Big flat cakes of ice bobbed in the black, swift water.

"We must make a raft," Christopher said. "It is the only way we will be able to cross."

They worked all day to build the raft. The sun had just set when they finished.

They poled the raft into the black water. The swift current carried them downstream. Suddenly the raft lurched. George slipped.

"Look out!" shouted Christopher.

It was too late. George was thrown into the icy water. He caught the raft just in time. It took all his strength to pull himself back on. The raft swept on toward land. It was a little island.

They could not go on. The long, cold night closed in. The first gray daylight brought a welcome sight. The river had frozen over. The ice was thick enough to hold them. They walked to the other shore.

Ten miles further on they came to a lonely trader's house. There was a warm fire and hot food. George borrowed horses. "We must ride fast," George told Christopher. "We must tell the Governor that the French mean war."

Chapter 4

Indian Fighters

Governor Dinwiddie talked to George about the French plans. "I am sending you back to the Ohio country," Governor Dinwiddie told George. "This time you must take soldiers. We will build a fort at the head of the Ohio River."

George and his men marched toward the river. Indians brought bad news. The French had already built a fort there. Now France controlled the Ohio country.

George knew he could not defeat the French. They were too strong. Indians were helping them. George built a little fort, and called it Fort Necessity.

Early one morning the crack of French rifles cut the air. The battle lasted all day. George did not have enough men. Finally he had to surrender.

"Your soldiers can go free," the French commander told George. "But they must leave the Ohio country." Washington and his men began the slow march back to Virginia.

People welcomed George home. They knew he had fought bravely.

Soon George heard that more soldiers had arrived from England. They would help fight the French. An Englishman, General Braddock, was their commander.

George helped guide Braddock's army west over the mountains. The soldiers were nearing the French fort when the French and Indians struck. They opened fire from the tall grass and from behind trees and rocks. Savage Indian war cries rang through the air. The English soldiers fired back, but they could not see the enemy.

A French bullet ripped George's hat. Two more bullets cut through his uniform. Twice his horses were shot and killed.

The English soldiers lost the battle. Sadly, the army retreated to Virginia.

George was unhappy about losing the battle. But, for a special reason, he was glad to be home. He often called on a pretty young widow.

Her name was Martha Custis. Martha smiled up at the tall, young colonel when they danced. "I think you are happier on a horse than on the dance floor," Martha teased him. George was falling in love.

The war with France was not over. Once more the English and the men from Virginia marched against the French fort. General Forbes was their commander. He asked George to lead the Virginia soldiers.

The long march ended in victory for the English. The French burned their fort and fled. England had control of the Ohio country at last.

As soon as the English had won, George went back home. Pretty Martha Custis was waiting.

Chapter 5

Mount Vernon

The day was January 6, 1759. Cheerful fires burned in the Custis house. There was a hum of voices and laughter. Then there was quiet as the minister married George and Martha. Young Colonel Washington smiled down happily at his bride.

A busy new life began for George. He had been away from Mount Vernon too long. "Every barn and fence and shed needs repairing," he told Martha.

George was happy with his new family. Martha's first husband had died leaving her with two children. Jackie was four years old, and a little girl, Patsy, was two years younger. Jackie and Patsy made Mount Vernon a lively place.

Soon Jackie was old enough to ride with his stepfather. "He will be a good horseman," George told Martha. "I can teach him to ride with me in the fox hunts. He will like that."

Patsy liked music. George gave her a new piano. "As for myself I do not know one note from another," George said. But in the evening he liked to sit in the candlelight and hear Patsy play.

The happy days at Mount Vernon lasted fifteen years. George made Mount Vernon a large, successful plantation. He became one of the important men of Virginia.

He was elected to the Virginia House of Burgesses. The Burgesses made most of the laws for the colony. England made the others. George learned what laws worked best. He learned how to plan new laws.

Trouble was beginning for Virginia and the other colonies. England made laws the colonists believed would take away their freedom. The colonists hated the English taxes most of all.

"It is unfair for England to make us pay taxes," George said to Martha.

"We do not have men to represent us in the English government."

The angry colonists sent men to a meeting in Philadelphia. "We will try to make England change the laws," they said. The meeting was called the Continental Congress. George was one of the men chosen to go from the colony of Virginia.

England would not listen to the colonies. "There may be war," George told Martha. "Many Americans say we must fight for our rights."

The quarrel with England became worse. Sharp fighting broke out in Massachusetts. English soldiers took over Boston. American soldiers camped outside the city. They were brave fighters, but they were not an army.

They needed to learn to march and work and fight together. They needed officers. And they needed a general.

Congress knew Washington was a good soldier. They knew he could lead men. Congress named George Washington as General of the first American army.

George was sad to leave his family. He wrote to Martha, "My dearest. I would find more happiness in one month with you in Mount Vernon than in 50 years at war. But the American cause is being put under my care."

Chapter 6

The Trap

Washington worked hard to train the army. He appointed officers. He tried to get enough food and guns.

It took months to get the big guns the army needed. Washington wanted to attack the British in Boston. "Put the cannons on the highest hills," he ordered.

The men worked silently under a cold winter moon. At dawn the British saw the cannons. They knew American gunners could blast the city. The British did not have enough men. They sailed away from Boston.

"The British will go on fighting," Washington told his men. "We must be ready to meet their next attack. I believe it will be at New York." Washington marched his men south over the dusty roads.

Washington had guessed right. Early one morning in New York, an excited messenger came running. "British ships are coming, sir, one after the other."

By night almost 100 English ships were off New York. For days the enemy ships kept coming. They were carrying more than 30,000 soldiers.

"Our army is much smaller than the British," Washington told his men. "But we must defend New York."

Important news came from the Continental Congress in Philadelphia.

Congress had passed the Declaration of Independence on July 4, 1776. The Declaration said the American colonies were free from England.

"Read the Declaration to all the soldiers," Washington ordered. "Now they will know their country depends on them." The soldiers roared out their cheers. They had been fighting for their rights. Now they were fighting for something more important—their independence.

The English attacked on Long Island across the wide East River. The battle lines formed. Washington stayed with his men. The fight began. Bullets whined through the trees and bushes. Shouts rang out above the crack of rifle fire. Bayonets flashed.

Rifle butts swung like clubs. American and British blood soaked the ground. Quiet bodies lay where men had fallen.

The American army fought bravely, but they were beaten. The army retreated to the forts Washington had built in the hills above the East River. New York was across the river.

"We must act quickly or we will be trapped," Washington said. "The English warships will sail up the river and block us from New York."

Washington sent for every small boat within miles. That night he ordered his men to the shore.

Through the dark night, sweating men rowed the little boats back and forth to New York. All through the night Washington stood by the river.

Sometimes he gave an order. Always the men saw his tall figure.

Morning came. Fog covered the hills and the river. Not a sound came from the American forts.

"Send out scouts," ordered the English commander. Soon the scouts ran back with the news. Every American was gone! Washington's army had broken out of the trap.

Washington had saved his army. But he was not strong enough to defeat the British. The British drove the Americans out of New York. They drove them from the rocky hills beyond the city. They followed them across New Jersey. Washington and his army retreated across the Delaware River into Pennsylvania.

Chapter 7

Victory or Death

The cold, dark days of early winter began. The British general thought the fighting was over for the winter. He sent many of his soldiers back across New Jersey to New York City.

Washington's soldiers were weak and ragged. Americans were discouraged. It seemed they could never win now. But Washington gave a new password, *"Victory or Death."*

It was six o'clock on Christmas evening, 1776. The Americans waited in the darkness for orders to march. A driving snow stung their faces.

The men moved slowly across the slippery snow to the bank of the Delaware River. They climbed into small boats. Floating ice filled the dark river.

Washington crossed the river. He stood on the shore. His cloak was wrapped closely around him against the bitter cold. He gave his orders quietly. "Keep your soldiers together," he told his officers. "Build fires to keep them warm. There is a long march ahead."

It was late night before all the soldiers were finally across the river.

Washington called his officers together. "Tell the men we will attack at Trenton," Washington said. "We will surprise the enemy."

The men began the slow, cold march. Many soldiers had only rags for shoes. Their cut, bruised feet left blood on the snow.

By daylight the Americans were at Trenton. Hessian soldiers were there. They were hard-fighting men from Germany. Their Prince had paid them to fight for the British.

The first crack of rifle shots brought the Hessians tumbling from their houses. The officers did not have time to tell their men what to do. "Fire!" they shouted. The Hessians tried to fire. But it was too late.

American cannonballs and bullets were already splintering the walls of the houses and smashing through the windows. The Hessians surrendered.

Washington had captured Trenton. Americans cheered the news. "We can fight back! We can win!" they told each other.

Washington thought the Americans could win another victory. But it was time for many of the men to go home. They had promised to be soldiers only for a short time. Now they wanted to leave. Washington knew he must keep his men fighting. "Call the men together," he ordered.

General Washington rode his horse slowly along the lines of ragged men. His tall figure towered in the saddle.

"You have done all I asked you to do and more," he said to them. "But your country is at stake, your wives, your homes, and everything you love. You have worn yourselves out. But I do not know how to spare you. Stay one month longer, and you will serve your country in a way you never can again."

The drums rolled. Then there was silence. One by one, the soldiers stepped forward. They would stay. Washington had saved his army for another battle.

Chapter 8

Valley Forge

Washington attacked next at the little town of Princeton. The fight was short and savage. Washington was in the thick of the battle. A young officer who was near him wrote home to his wife, *"I shall never forget what I felt when I saw Washington brave all the dangers with a thousand deaths flying around him."*

The British line broke and their soldiers ran. Washington shouted to his men, *"It is a fine fox chase, my boys!"* The Americans raced to take prisoners.

Washington's men had stayed with him for the battle. But now many of them went home. The colonies would send new soldiers in the spring. Washington tried to hold what was left of his small army together. Sometimes he felt as if there were no hope.

"How we shall be able to rub along till the new Army is raised, I know not," he wrote.

Washington was sure the English would attack when good weather began. He must be patient and wait.

Finally the British moved against Philadelphia. Once again Washington tried to keep the British from taking an important American city. Once again Washington lost. The British took Philadelphia in the autumn.

"We must camp outside Philadelphia for the winter," Washington wrote to Congress. He chose a place called Valley Forge.

The cold weather set in. Snow fell. Icy winds blew across the hills. The shivering American soldiers tried to keep warm. They cut logs and built cabins. There was only green wood to burn. There were not enough blankets. The soldiers' clothes and shoes were worn out. Many men were in rags.

There was almost no food. The soldiers had a bitter joke. *"What's for dinner, sir?"* The answer was always, *"Fire cake and water."* Fire cake was a rough bread cooked over a campfire. Many men became weak and sick. Many died.

The long months seemed without hope. But day after day men lived on. They knew Washington was with them. Soldiers on guard in the cold, lonely night watched for his tall figure. The men waited for his word of greeting. Then somehow they felt better. "We will win," they said.

Washington did not lose hope. He worked to keep his men alive. He asked the governors of the colonies to send food and clothes and blankets.

But he knew something else was needed for the army.

"Our soldiers must have better training," Washington told his officers. The officers worked long days drilling the soldiers. "Forward! Fire! Charge!" The commands rang across the hardpacked snow on the drill field. The men learned to move quickly in answer to orders.

The warm days of spring came at last. The men had better clothes and food. Most important, they were trained soldiers.

On April 30, 1778, exciting news came. A messenger galloped into camp bringing a letter from Congress. The letter said that France would help the colonies. Washington called his officers.

"Tell the men we do not fight alone," he said. "France will help us."

When the soldiers heard the news, cheers rang through the camp. Now there was real hope for America to win.

Washington ordered a parade. The soldiers were thin. Their clothes were patched. But they put dogwood flowers in their hats. They marched with their heads high. Their lines were straight. Their step was quick.

George Washington watched the soldiers proudly. They had lived through the bitter, killing winter of Valley Forge. Now they were trained to fight.

Chapter 9

By Land and by Sea

In late May a spy came into Washington's camp with good news. "The British are getting ready to leave Philadelphia," he said.

The British knew the American army was getting stronger. They also knew French ships and soldiers were on their way to help the Americans. They decided to retreat to New York. The British soldiers marched from Philadelphia, across New Jersey. Burning heat settled down.

"This is our chance to attack," Washington said.

The Americans attacked the British near the village of Monmouth. The sharp crack of American rifles cut through the blanket of heat. The fight was on.

The battle raged all day. Now the training of Valley Forge showed. The Americans fought the big British army to a standstill. The British retreated to New York. Slowly the tide of the war was turning.

Still the British army stayed in New York. The British fleet was in the harbor.

"We dare not attack New York," Washington wrote to Congress. "We are not strong enough."

Months went by before Washington was ready to attack again. Then he went south to Virginia. The British had another big army there commanded by Lord .Cornwallis.

Washington saw his chance for victory. "Our soldiers will attack by land," he told his officers. "The French are helping us. Their fleet will close in from the sea."

The Americans and the French trapped Cornwallis at Yorktown. The roar of the cannon began. Shell after shell ripped into the British lines. There was no way for the British army to escape. On October 19, 1781, the British surrendered.

Washington ordered his soldiers to stand along the road from Yorktown.

It was a warm sunny day. Washington rode to the head of the line. His thoughts went back over the six long years of war. He remembered the hard marches and the bitter defeats. He remembered the soldiers who had died. Now a powerful British army was surrendering. It was a great victory for America.

Drums beat in the distance. The British were marching out of Yorktown. Washington heard the first sounds from the British band. For a moment he smiled. The band was playing *The World Turned Upside Down*.

Washington watched the British soldiers pile their rifles on the ground.

The war dragged on for two more years. But the real fighting was over.

Peace came at last. The thirteen colonies were free. They were now the United States of America.

The last English soldiers left New York in November of 1783. Now Washington could go home.

On December 4, Washington said good-by to his officers at Fraunces' Tavern in New York. The eight long years of work and struggle were over. Washington looked at his officers and said, *"With a heart full of love and gratitude I now take leave of you."*

One by one Washington's officers came to him and shook his hand. At the last they had no words to say. There were tears in their eyes. There were tears in Washington's eyes too.

Chapter 10

The First President

On his first day at home Washington was up early. His favorite horse, Nelson, was saddled and waiting for him. Washington rode fast over Mount Vernon's frozen fields. It was dinner-time before he came back.

"All the years I was away I made plans for making Mount Vernon better," Washington told Martha. "Now we can begin."

Life at Mount Vernon was busy, but Washington did not forget his country. He worried about the new government. He knew it did not have enough power to rule the country.

Finally the new states sent men to Philadelphia to plan a better government. Washington was one of the men from Virginia.

Each man at the meeting had his own plans about what to do. "We need someone to lead the meeting," Benjamin Franklin said. "Otherwise we will be crowing out our ideas like a barnyard of roosters." The men elected George Washington to be their leader.

This meeting in Philadelphia was called the Constitutional Convention.

The men planned a new and stronger government. They wrote down the powers it should have. They called this the *Constitution of the United States*.

The Constitution said there should be a Congress to make laws, and courts to settle arguments about what laws mean. The Constitution also said there should be a President to head the government. He was to carry out the laws Congress made. The people knew the one man they trusted most. They elected George Washington as their first President.

Washington was sad to leave Mount Vernon. He was 53 years old. But the country needed him. He became the first President on April 30, 1789.

The capital of the United States was then New York. There was a big parade down the city streets. The harbor was crowded with ships flying their flags. A 21-gun salute was fired. Soldiers marched. People cheered when they saw Washington's big yellow coach drawn by cream-colored horses.

There had never been a President before. "How will he act?" the people asked.

Some were afraid the President would turn into a king. *"Fine folk would spoil our General, if they could,"* one old soldier wrote. *"He never was a greater man than when he rode among us with his dusty boots."*

But people soon stopped worrying. Washington did not act like a king.

He did not try to run the country alone. He asked other leaders for their ideas. He chose the best people in the country to help him. He took trips North and South. He wanted to find out what the people were thinking.

There had never been a government like the United States. Washington knew everything the government did was important for the future. He planned his actions carefully. He had to make the new government work.

America began to grow. Factories hummed in the new nation. Farm crops filled the big barns. George Washington had led his country in war. Now he led it in peace.

Chapter *11*

"First in War, First in Peace"

Washington served four years as the President. Then the people elected him President again. The capital was now in Philadelphia.

Washington found the United States had many new problems. People did not always agree about what to do. They were beginning to form two political parties.

Alexander Hamilton and Thomas Jefferson were two of the President's closest advisers. They led the new parties. Each man argued for his own ideas. Soon they became bitter enemies.

"I wish Hamilton and Jefferson would work together," Washington said. "They both want the best for the country, and I need them both."

Soon Washington had to face another problem. The new government needed money. Congress passed tax laws. One law made people pay a tax for making whisky. Men in western Pennsylvania were angry.

"Down with the tax!" they cried. "We will fight before we pay it!" The men got out their guns.

"This tax is an important test," Washington said. "The laws of the United States must be obeyed."

Washington called for United States soldiers. Once again men in uniform made the long march over the mountains to western Pennsylvania. The revolt ended without a battle.

Washington also had to deal with troubles abroad. France and England were at war. Many Americans wanted to help France. They remembered how France had helped America win her freedom from England.

President Washington spoke for the country. "We fought for our independence," he said. "We must stay independent. We are not strong enough yet to help other countries."

Many people were angry, but George Washington stood firm.

There was trouble with Spain too. Spain held the port of New Orleans at the mouth of the Mississippi River. Spain would not let ships from the United States use the river to trade with other countries.

Washington sent Thomas Pinckney to settle the troubles with Spain. He waited anxiously for news.

Washington's birthday, February 22, 1796, gave him a chance to forget his worries. The country celebrated the President's birthday. Church bells rang. Cannons were fired. Crowds flocked to the President's house. Martha had punch and cake ready for everyone.

During the day good news arrived that a treaty with Spain was signed. "This is the best birthday present of all," Washington told Martha. "Spain says that Americans may now use all of the Mississippi River. People in the West will cheer this news."

There was still trouble with England. Washington sent John Jay to England to make a treaty. Jay made the best treaty he could. But many Americans believed it was not fair to the United States. They said America should fight England. They blamed Washington and Jay for the treaty.

"We cannot listen to the angry voices," Washington said. "The treaty will keep us at peace. We must have peace to grow strong."

Most people trusted Washington to know what to do. Congress agreed to the treaty.

Washington was also busy planning a new capital city for the United States. Later the city was named *Washington* for the President.

President Washington finished his second term. Many people wanted him to be President again. "No," he said. "I believe it is time for another man." Washington's work was done.

On the move back to Mount Vernon, wagons carried the furniture. Martha insisted that the parrot and their pet dog, Vulcan, ride in the carriage with them. The parrot screamed. Vulcan barked. "It sounds like a battlefield," George said with a smile.

Washington went home to Mount Vernon and the life he and Martha loved. In the long days of spring Washington was up with the sun. He watched the work being done on Mount Vernon's buildings. "There is the music of hammers and the smell of paint everywhere," he wrote to a friend.

Washington rode over the farms of Mount Vernon. He planned the crops. He watched the wheat fields ripen and the young colts racing in the pastures.

Martha's grandchildren, George and Nelly Custis, were growing up. Their laughter brightened the house. *"I have never a dull or lonesome hour, never find a day too long,"* Nelly wrote to a friend.

On Washington's birthday, 1799, there was a happy wedding at Mount Vernon. Nelly Custis was married to Washington's nephew, Lawrence Lewis. Guests filled the bright rooms. Washington watched proudly. The pretty bride gave him a happy smile.

The year neared its end. One cold day in December, 1799, Washington went riding through the fields. A winter storm broke. Washington was wet and cold when he reached home. His hair was caked with ice.

That evening he felt sick. During the night he could hardly breathe. Martha knew he was desperately sick. The doctors came. They did their best, but the next evening George Washington was dead.

Americans mourned. Washington had led them to victory and freedom. He had been their first President. "He was the father of our country," people said.

One of Washington's old soldiers remembered him with these great words. The words have lived across the years. George Washington was *"first in war, first in peace, and first in the hearts of his countrymen."*